Pra

"Coutley's riveting new collection spirals around the complexities of host as multitude or throng, host as spiritual sustenance, host as living organism upon which a parasite lives. These poems, dazzling in their heartbreak, slice themselves open along the razor's edge of risk and tenderness. Here, patriarchal violence and the desire to subjugate women are paralleled by the deliberate ecocide of the Anthropocene. Here, the desires and impossibilities of nurturing are pitted against the desires and impossibilities of the synthetic object. These are unforgettable, achingly gorgeous, sunflower-studded poems that 'scream for a brightness none of us can hold.'"—**Lee Ann Roripaugh, author of *Tsunami vs. the Fukushima 50***

"Host—what does it mean? This is the crucial question of Lisa Fay Coutley's searing new collection of poetry. What is it to be a mother hosting sons, especially in a nation in the grip of patriarchal rage? To have a female body forced to host violence and trauma? To be part of the human host destroying our host, the earth? These are deeply lived and deeply felt questions for Coutley, who brings them under her fierce gaze and writes them into poems of great candor and power."—**Dana Levin, author of *Now Do You Know Where You Are***

"Part elegy to the Anthropocene, part case study of internet-era loneliness, the metaphorical relationships woven throughout *Host*'s poignant, timely, and necessary poems are many: mother host to son, woman host to patriarchy, flower host to human pleasure, Earth host to people's waste. Among these layered threats to the body and the planet, there's a plea for repair, for reclamation, as one speaker asks, 'did you hear me / agree to be an island?' Here we have a poet at the height of her craft, skillfully rendering the essential dispatches we all need to hear."—**Trey Moody, author of *Autoblivion***

"Coutley's *Host* pushes Rilke's closures to new ones: to the edges of the contemplative and fervent: 'Would you change your life if you knew / corn growing sounds like a limb slipping / through a sleeve?' Coutley drops us into the most deft, poignant, and serious stakes to see our contemporary lives clearly, succumbing to the attentive as a possible way through. Inside a human 'constant state of ache' is her astute lyric that crafts the many selves one can have inside an image. In this is a valiant pursuit of an ominous present-state and afterlife for the human, the earth, and the forgone retrievals that carry and haunt: 'Body of our bodies, we are becoming / strangers.' Here in the poem 'Why to Save the World,' we learn how estrangement is at the center of our burning questions. *Host* is full of these important insights and Coutley anchors us with a dictum that can become a refrain: 'When trying to change the world, / go that bold.' This collection insists on it, to which I am grateful for the luminosity in her and in these pages."—**Prageeta Sharma, author of *Grief Sequence***

HOST

LISA FAY COUTLEY

The University of Wisconsin Press

Publication of this book has been made possible, in part,
through support from the Brittingham Trust.

The University of Wisconsin Press
728 State Street, Suite 443
Madison, Wisconsin 53706
uwpress.wisc.edu

Gray's Inn House, 127 Clerkenwell Road
London EC1R 5DB, United Kingdom
eurospanbookstore.com

Printed in the United States of America
This book may be available in a digital edition.
Library of Congress Cataloging-in-Publication Data

Names: Coutley, Lisa Fay, author.
Title: Host / Lisa Fay Coutley.
Other titles: Wisconsin poetry series.
Description: Madison, Wisconsin : The University of Wisconsin Press, 2024. |
Series: Wisconsin poetry series
Identifiers: LCCN 2023031035 | ISBN 9780299347147 (paperback)
Subjects: LCGFT: Poetry.
Classification: LCC PS3603.O88823 H67 2024 | DDC 811/.6—dc23/eng/20230829
LC record available at https://lccn.loc.gov/2023031035

Contents

HOST

Independence Day

If the baby bird

                I save
one day

                          is wings

      apart

& facedown
& black
flies
in the neighbor's backyard

                      the next

we are both / a short lesson / in love's risk

& I want
        no one
to be forgiven.

Why to Save the World

We need to begin by shooting
       people, leaders who lead
       by a leash the property

they call theirs, a friend says. My son
       wants me to carry a little
       pistol because men still

haven't learned that I am my own
       smoking embers to tend.
       At this table with my bean burger

& dark beer I am more still than I've been
       in months, even when I wonder
       which of the sadfaced boys

passing in their hunt for Pokémon
       might be the one to hold
       a jagged blade to my throat.

I'm trying to remember how it felt
       to walk so close beside someone
       you let a bit of your weight fall

to them. Alone, you always listen
        to the new couple or old friends
        & feel them lie to each other,

performing themselves. I still hear
        the scream from the woman
        in the front row wearing the

president's brains after the sound
        the gun makes saves the silence
        from itself. We are all worried

we've forgotten something. One man
        leaves his drink at the bar & never
        wonders when he comes back if

someone drugged him while he pissed.
        Our hearts beating, our lungs
        pumping—we think of them as

often as we think how miles of asphalt
        might feel like duct tape
        over your gagged mouth.

On this birthday I wish to be invisible
        & to make this row full of men
        own my body, make them feel

living with a leash no one sees, tethered
            to threat. I don't want to forget
            my mother died on a bathroom

floor or to pretend our Earth is not
            in a constant state of ache—
            a body in pain being a body

under control. The gunshot echoes again.
            Who would we shoot first? What
            happens to a face the bullet owns?

How can a woman drink so much
            vodka her daughter could pass
            her on the street & never know?

Body of our bodies, we are becoming
            strangers. We each live at the edge
            of a wall we should never look over.

Anxiety

according to my therapist, is my body's / way of saying I'm a gazelle, head
bent / to long grass, eating but heeding the puma / who's tracking me, so
I often stop, raise my / face & wait, unable to chew until my brain / scans
the landscape to see I'm free / from teeth. In the tall window of this / office,
Lucinda the magenta orchid screams / or flames or celebrates even though it
is / January & there is no sky. There's an elephant / straight ahead, Buddha
to the left, a trampoline behind me / where once I rocked myself still for the
dull pain / in my pelvis. There are two silent clocks / & no foul smells, no
reason to fear this room / wants to hold me by my wrists / still light pours in
from the north / when a man's hand erases a girl's thigh / until she's the fish
with a fluke for its will / forcing her to flash her shimmering fins / bald at
the water's top for some lucky bird / come pluck her my parasite inside / I'll
be the bird flying a half life / singing against my own desire.

II.

Or I am not a gazelle. I am pinned
to the bed in a way only one of us likes.

I am breath locked behind the wire
drawn ribs of knowing you're running

out of this week's money to feed
your babies. I am learning to cry

quietly so as not to hurt everyone
around me. Each year I grow more

sunflowers for the faces I'm holding
underwater inside me. A bird of prey

in the house is one less in the sky.

Synthetic Love

I. *In England*

In case the car starts on fire
while he's hang gliding, Everard
pins a note to his love's chest
so no one dies trying to save her.
After their morning fuck, she lies
with her sleeping face on
while he winds the clock
in his dead mum's room.

II. *In Michigan*

Synthetic love activist Davecat
just wants to rub his wife's feet
in early morning light, but *organic
women are not constant*. Shi-chan is
the anchor that keeps him stable
in their room above his parents'
garage. When he crates his wife
to be shipped for repair, he kisses
both hands & cries he'll miss her.

III. *In Virginia*

Gordon has three guns & two girls / one of which fires as fast as you can /
pull the trigger. A woman in stilettos / & a thong is meat someone else has /
chewed & spit back on God's plate. / He wants his dolls buried / in the same
box as him / so they can become one dust.

IV. *In California*

Slade the repairman's running out of vaginas
& teeth again. *Sex is like a violent act*, he says,
but these dolls can take *a lot of physical abuse.*

V. *In Texas*

Michael is grateful for his harem
of eight top-heavy dolls & the Swedes
who are willing to sell real pubic hair
for when his ladies wear out. In this *high
form of masturbation* he does not want
to be seen as a *pervert*, but when he
wakes at 3 a.m. *with a raging hard-on*
he goes to the garage, grabs his doll
of choice, & goes at it. He *can't do that
with a woman*, he notes. *She can say no.*

VI. *At Abyss Creations, USA*

Receptionist Debbie says men are fifty
& balding & never going to get women
who look like this, who totally love them.
Doll Creator Matt feels best about men
who've made that emotional connection—
I've changed their lives for the better . . . like *insoles
in their shoes.* These men come home from work
excited to see their doll, & the *food bill's way cheaper.*

Rootbound

What I know of plants, I learned
from a woman whose name means
beauty, so of course the world wanted
to strip her of it. Always, there will
be a man whose hunger sharpens
a girl's softest parts into every edge
she'll bruise against. Roots do as roots
do, reaching down & out until it's clear
they've hit bottom & have no choice
but to push back, searching for more
soil, I guess. If some of my best lessons
came from men—why must I struggle
to see my grown sons among them (often
I mistype *sins* instead)? Why can't I accept
I can no longer talk them off the once was
stage of teenage drama (see those needles?
that redhot glass?)? If my father saw me
small once I wasn't he never cradled
my face & made it clear, & years later
I'm still sorry he never insisted on that
father-daughter dance, & I'd like him to
know, since he fell into eternity from a
toilet seat, still the dead deer on every
highway seem strained as if mid-dance
or as if they are trying so hard to see
better from where they are now & no

I don't frighten easily or run from love
or every nice guy but was gifted sense
enough to know when to shoot myself
from the sky, throw myself to my knees,
so I have no choice but to rise & keep
going, & maybe it's as simple as knowing
the container that holds you binds you
& reaching for more is reaching for end.

Learning Not to Want

I.

My body is its own apology
which cannot stop me from wanting
to drown the small girl inside me
building sturdier walls with fewer tools.

II.

The Internet says, in a past life
I fell from a church tower in 537 AD.
I was good, loved, missed by many.
This life, they say, will be longer though
I will watch all the others fall before me.

III.

I love best the man whose face
I always forget, yet he crowds all
the stars from my sky. My heart
is sick with billboards & road rage.

IV.

We all want unconditional love from someone
other than the dog, who promises only
to break your heart by no longer being
the face at the edge of the bed. So what

V.

if I never want to forget my mother
died on a bathroom floor. Most toads
die inside window wells. In truth,
the lullaby was always a muted wish.

VI.

In movies, it will begin with babies
no longer crying in their cribs, kids
missing, swing sets rusted still. No one
dreamed it could start with a poacher
killed by an elephant & devoured
by lions & the irony of real news.

VII.

In the 21st century, everyone watches
the world burn with the phantom

feeling of a hose in both hands
but no close water source.

VIII.

We post photos so every best friend
we've never met knows life continues
to reinvent itself, begging to be
called by another name, giving
someone else's number, which is
always up before yours.

IX.

Finally we decided to feel wounded
by everything to keep pretending to feel
something once our phones never rang
& there was nothing left to say, as if
without a pen the moon was useless.

A Son Might Say

It's about time you got a muffin
top yeah no stop my god you are
conceited don't take everything
so personally ugh why should you
get special treatment why can't you
just not do that why would anyone
eat that why would you wish for it
what will you do with flower petals
take them home and watch them rot
I didn't buy them for you they are
hers you should let her throw them
in the garbage if she wants to mom
he is not your baby you drive me
crazy oh look the car seat is now
a beer holder this is not going to be
a habit what did I tell you duh that is
exactly why I don't tell you anything
have you learned nothing from this
week if someone looks unhappy
leave him alone you never know
when to shut up no he's my baby
I'll hold him I'll change his diaper
I'll feed him you're doing it wrong
should I do it like this why would I
not ask you of course I love you
you're my mother if you ask again

I'm going to hit you why do you ask
stupid questions are you dumb as fuck
yeah sleep well see you in the morning
drive safe call me if you need anything

To the Friend Who Sent Me Goodwill Forks as a Gift

I'm not embarrassed to live alone
with my three mismatched forks.

I'm not sorry you had to wash one
to eat the omelet I fried for you.

I want you to wait until your son
is asleep, then quiet into his room

to his bed's edge & try to see him
without that cosmic nightlight

inside him, in a now that does not
involve you. As they do, my sons

outgrew me & the home-cooked
meals I might throw in their faces

for the way a single mother grinds
her teeth to pieces in broken sleep.

I'm breath locked behind wiredrawn
ribs. The dark welt of alone. Blemish

even to women like you who believe

they know what going it alone means.
Co-parenting. I keep waiting for
this dark fist in my chest to pearl.

I could be baptized a second time
just to let someone hold my weight.

God, how we ruin you with words,
though we like the rhyme of saying

meth den or *meth head* in theory
even if I'm cursed to see a hive

of bodies pulsating around the same
hanging dime. You cannot possibly

dream there'll be a time when you will
be asked to wrap your spare silverware

& mail it to your son in his new city,
his new place, his new him, the sweet

smell of yellow smoke the only warm
blanket around his shaking frame.

Blocked

My therapist says I'm starting little fires / everywhere completely unironically / controlled emotional burn we giggle / jinx personal potshots / blocked contacts for $200 / please / goodbye white guy who talks over me / & white guy who I tell about white guy who talks over me / talks over me to say why white guy / is such a dick inserting his own / joke about stopping me to mansplain / block / blockblock / The world is going to get a whole lot smaller / that way she reminds me as if / I give a fuck about having / to take my turn as the moon. / The desk flat against my face understands / what loneliness does / & doesn't taunt me over its glasses. / I just wanted the one / whose face I always forget / to know there are more viruses / than stars in this universe that / a fluke makes a grasshopper think it can swim / & tweens want plastic surgery to look like themselves / through a Snapchat filter / .

Sunflowers, 2020

One hundred this season, each with rust
　　　　or wilt or whatever anger waits
　　　　until you bloom to take you down

the same day. Everyone I've ever loved
　　　　as much as I do the drama
　　　　of saying so. Healing hinges

on believing the hope inside Earth
　　　　will open inside you without
　　　　a side of machete. This year

for isolation I sowed mammoth walls
　　　　so overcrowded I could see
　　　　it is the way it has always been

done, sick with too many things to Google
　　　　yet still—their faces bloom bigger
　　　　than dinner plates shot through

with sun. What are we—to believe in sin
　　　　as an invention separate of us.
　　　　Blocks away live music is playing

a face I once loved & had finally forgotten
to miss. An entire summer spent
worrying tongue over molars over

masks & hips that simply can't not dance.
I tried to pressure wash the virus
from more than three thousand

leaves breathing above me. I let a single
stink bug live for the world
before us engraved on its back.

I miss you so much I made a junk drawer
corner of yard where weak plants
go untended. There is a sadness

packed storm-tight inside our bones—
a hope for more, the memory of
being the first star or the darkness

before it. I miss you so much when
I fill the watering can I hold
the hose head under

until it struggles   then doesn't.

The Killing Game

I never knew if I loved anyone
until a truck ran them down or
a revolver went off in my mind
& I could picture myself splayed
over the kitchen's linoleum floor
or frowning slightly & shrugging
to go. Once I had my first son
& then my second, I knew what
missing meant—first the girl
who never held herself but
held them, & then the woman
they would never let hold them
ever again. Time has wide teeth
in the meat of us, we know, but
after I imagined my second son
dead of exposure or my first by
overdose or both by someone
else's hand, I could see my own
locked around someone's throat
or pressing a razor against my vein
until I saw myself old & alone then
never old, & the killing, the missing
game became boys trying to know
how to let the Lake take my bones.
When a mother dies, everything her
child does after is a wish, so now

that my sons are grown I want to
offer to go last, to let them pass
through the world without alone
like smoke soaked into the walls
of their oldest home. The Earth
will hold them then & never stop
showing us all new ways to hurt
ourselves & each other, & how
could any mother really blame her
for hoping that we will leave her
first, so we'll never need to find
ways to survive time without her.

What of the Mother

who doesn't love her children
more than herself. *You got me*
fucked up, my son says when I say

anything wrong as a bedroom closet
in a kitchen. What's a woman
when she won't grease the pan

& hold her hand to it? What's aching
land to do? To see oil in an ocean
as blood coloring a sudsless tub—

an open vein the way pain razors
out—you'd need to believe Earth
could send some unloved sons

into deep sea with inevitable weapons
for hands, the same way an ant stands
poised on its blade of grass, praying

to be eaten for the parasite inside
its will. *Humans have never been made*
to devour one another, I say to the fish

looking up through the cloudy water
of yesterday's rain-dredged bottom
where I hunker with nothing

for their open mouths but my face
shaking back at me, *yet we do*. I'm sorry
the song is still lodged in our chests.

The fawn with the injured mother
has no choice but to grow under
the shadow of her wound.

Parasitism for Dummies

Sea lice eat salmon
alive where they are being
raised, so we can eat.

NOTE: *raised* is a verb humans use for the loving environment in which
they might nurture a child.

NOTE II: a salmon parasitized by lice is gray when filleted & painted to pass
as food.

NOTE X: what goes unsaid is the shipful of men enslaving the ship full
of boys forced to drag a courthouse-sized net over the ocean floor,
like razing forest.

Unpopular Opinion Game:
A Pantheist's Approach to Revelations

I love to
make stories says the ex-priest
        who knows how to fuck me

but never lets himself
cum. *I love you* means I would
        wear his poisoned coat

        for him knowing
he'll always insist on hoarding his hurt.
        I understand. The glass she

chewed way back when is just beginning
      to cut me.   Now.
        One third

of Earth's water is oil. A great star
    fell from reality TV & was gifted
        the key to the bottomless alone.

Pitted light. Diminished
day. We breathe

six feet apart cross-legged watching God
        gnaw

his little cage. Sackcloth sackcloth sky & hair
or some other sacred

                              before we were made
          to suck blood from the water or shame
from the blood.

                              What seven thunders
utter I want to ask you what tongue quakes
          the spine of a mountain range

what hail
churns oceans to a rolling boil
                    what missing

                    tells time's smell & begs the exit
                              wound to reinvent itself.

Letter to the Aftermath

There was a time before this screen
though our bodies only remember it
like a room with a wall where once
there were portholes. Light no longer
falling over some lovers slouched
shoulders in the tub. I made a garden
& still I wasn't happy—one hundred
sunflowers & the only screaming
I heard was mine. A hole, core deep.
A detonation waiting. The morning
I felt most lost from myself I could
no longer hear my plants in bloom.
I erased my Someday list. Clouds were
just clouds. I tried to remind myself
crows won't eat their dead. Instead
they gather around a body in silence
or raucous. Whether you believe they
grieve there, sometimes moments
sometimes days, or you believe they
gather data to avoid their own demise
says everything your family needs
to know about you. I believe Earth
will be the last mammoth to flower,
who decided one chance to weapon
her beauty is simply not enough.
What if that is the only story

we have to tell you, the voice
of our planet so quiet inside us
we could never see her breathing
from space is a heart beating
& it was always going
to be too late.

September 1, 2019

I lie back flat on our wooden deck
next to my dog surrounded by heavy
headed sunflowers hoping they'll seed
so I can see what can come from love
& devotion. I feel as silly as anyone does
wishing on this road where neighbors
filled a pothole & fingered *Trump 2020*
in Quikrete. *Waves of anger & fear circulate*
over the bright, you wrote eighty years ago
though I cannot report more than we
have worn the shore thinner, old friend.
& how can we expect less from water
in motion. Every grain of sand trying
to find its way back to ocean or origin.

To find your way back to a point of origin
you would need to read all fifteen quotes
that will change your life if you choose to
apply how migratory birds find their way
tethered to a nest & hopping on one leg,
according to Google search's suggestions.
Fuck evolution for Facebook: the safe place
to hate where once there were town squares
for open stoning. Someone's president says
we should pool our nuclear weapons because
it's hurricane season. Last week the *sun cracked*
open & a 2 million mph gust is set to lash Earth.
Make the best of it—bend your neck in awe
of Aurora Borealis—despite the sky's limit.

Even Aurora, goddess of dawn, is bound
by the call of an only sun. Rosy-fingered
bitch caught in her own kind of cycle.
Old habits formed from older pain,
mismanaged grief. Why must *we suffer*
them all again. Who among us recalls
coming home from a first day of school,
opening the door to find your parents
were suddenly in another country
you have never called home, the way
your backpack slumped against the wall
or you never took it off as no one
held you, rocked you, as you wept
to sleep into your newest always pain.

To sleep with your newest always pain
will require taking your medicine good
little until sleep is duty. Euphoric dream
we can't see us in your mirror anymore
though we've made a contest of staring.
Maybe we always did. We cannot stop
asking if there is not another, better,
easier reason we haven't found a cure
for Earth. Maybe it's as simple as looking
into that expired hope & repeating we
are the disease. Or is that too confusing
with so many heavy bets on the table?
We all know Earth could be flat if it were
not round. If we could agree on even that.

* *

What if we could agree Earth is not just
round but she knows more than us & so
knows the song you sing in the shower,
if you pray in vain to one or more gods
as you dig your nails into your lover's
ass & curl your toes back to forget who
you are & what happens in your dreams
is Earth's blurred cursive, a fractured map
showing you who you've been & could be.

Would you change your life if you knew
corn growing sounds like a limb slipping
through a sleeve? I need to be surrounded
by heavy-headed sunflowers to see them
scream for a brightness none of us can hold.

& why would we fear a scream we cannot
hear. So: Earth has a fever. She must cut
the virus' population. End stop. No cry

for help. We must each grieve the silence
of love. Just one memory of my mother
rubbing my temples might make it easier

to let night take my eyes. We wish for children
who'll treat us with tenderness on this planet's
asphalt & smashed glass as if hers is not a life

of impact, a body blasted from bodies fighting
for body. Lightning slices Earth 100x/second,
8 million/day. When she screams in darkness

she cannot hold, do you suppose she sees
us, on our knees, trying to crawl to safety?

To crawl to safety, cradle the darkness
inside yourself to sleep by designing
an inspiring meme using half a tree
bright with ripe berries set against white
winter. When trying to change the world,
go that bold. *I believe she sees herself*, I say,
though no one turns to listen or speak
because I'm alone.

     Dear Earth. Even my dog
bolted the deck for a squirrel trampolining
the sunflowers & J—emailed to say, Finally
he found love out there. I feel nothing
is the lie I tell the dirt because it'll remember
long after fire reclaims the whole lonely table:
loving you, loving me, could've been enough.

Crown

Tonight swims with raw root & nerve
exposed to stars & windchill. The living

room disappears. I go to the bathroom
to see myself reflected, to know I still exist

inside pain. Dear gentle dentist who offered
to numb me anytime, how could you let me be

so hungry. So dumb. Such stubborn blood
my father cut & drew for me again & again—

the same old story, same mean childhood
dentist, same red crayons chewed en route

from Catholic school to dreaded cleaning.
Swallow the thorn to become the thorn.

How many times did you tell me that story?
I only remember the last. So many Pabsts.

I imagine now, how carefully you married
your story to its glory, tonguing that bad

molar you'd been silencing with Tylenol
for weeks, until, midsentence, it was loose

enough to spit into your palm just as you
strutted through your past, chewing wax. So

tough. Or so you hoped the world would say
you down through time. Tonight I wish

you were here to walk me through this
strange pain, to tell me just how many hours

you stared into your hall of mirrors, rooting
out your softest spots behind their aches

before settling on the perfect moment to
excise, to cover with rage, to name it survive.

Oubliette

Father said the more love the more
    work & worry. Don't tell me again
        how another woman would have

known. Some secrets sit so still
    at the back of your knee. Hall
        leads to hallway. Ask me why

light can pour warm through a cold bay
    window while water under sun is dark
        as a closed door. A man's hand

erases a girl's thigh. The trees start starving
    themselves into everyone's favorite color.
        Her darkest room digs itself

below her throne. The body knows no
    wrong move. The more love, the more.

Psychodrama I: Middle-Aged Mother & Adult Son on Mount Baldy

Mother: Imagine a woman naked,
her knees bent stems exposed to the air
above the hot water of her soapy tub.

Son: Um, okay?

See her reading the *Duino Elegies*, weeping
for the house where she has lived alone
longer than it took Odysseus to get home.

stares over waves of autumn leaves

Can you imagine her?

Sure.

You can imagine such a woman?

Yeah, I said sure.

Can you imagine that naked weeping
woman is your mother & grasp that
before you passed through her body
she was a smaller angrier version of her
that had never wanted to dream
of your face braced in her hands?

points That's Lake George. & that's
where my friend shot the black bear
we couldn't track through the downpour.

Can you imagine her? I need you to
understand the impossible, to see me
as a body, to know that loneliness
for me means never feeling at ease
with another human, all of them dead
but you & you cannot see me for me.

Mom.

Always on, always in costume. When
I was a girl, I was afraid to pull the drain
& be taken through the tub to a place
I didn't know love or anyone's face.

You're driving the four-wheeler home.

I've never driven a four-wheeler.

You can learn.

I don't want to.

But you're going to.

You never listen to me. I said no
I don't want to drive a machine
that killed your dad. You don't listen.

You'll be fine. You're a good driver.

stares, heart heavy in its quick ticking

The two descend the mountain slow
for the moss grown over animal holes
& slate giving way to gravity as any body.

Did you hear anything I said, honey?

I heard you. This is the brake, reverse,
throttle, how to switch to four-wheel dig . . .

Honey, I said I don't want to . . .

Mom, you got this. Mom *looks into her
eyes* stay to the bank through the deepest
puddles. I'll be right behind you. Try
to have fun.

The woman sees herself younger, her arms
around the body of the boy she loved enough
to make this boy, who, like the first boy, is
forcing her to do something she doesn't want
to do. Leaves the color of rust, bruise, burning
closing in. The brown water parts before her

& the engine revs between her legs, uneasy
then steady, & she forgets to brake for safety,
muddy waves & laughter in her wake, her son
watching a woman's hair strain for bright sky.

Dear First Love—

When you said *hot* even though
your friends didn't think so loud

out the windows of their muscle
cars, I said, yes, please, another piece

of me field then street. When you said
can you feel how ready I am I stopped

hearing the song on Andy's boom box
& the delicate language of self while you

wrote a louder story I would sing
to be quiet, quieter inside me little

eclipse after avalanche. When you said *I
am so close,* I steadied my leg over the fire

learning to burn myself before you would
ever have to ask. Did you know—

first love—this dead decade later
as Redwoods are ravaged by scorching

science writes to say there's still hope
because such thick bark can thrive

even with deep burns. First boy who didn't
listen when I repeated *no* did you hear me

agree to be an island? I'm angry as sacred
earth. You said handcuff. I said charred

stretch of vein tangled in bird wrist
then let you nest your metal in me.

Reversion

Such as when a strange man opens / my dog's old knee to saw the bone in half / & lock it in place with metal, which (of course) / looks like a key, so he might walk again / pain free. I call him Mr. Martini in the clear / cone he learns he doesn't need to wear / if he puppy trails me room-to-room / & together / we resist licking our wounds. / Where they sliced him is a rough entrance in / to an ending I want not to touch / (how easy it would be to catch an edge & send him / into pain or past, which are his now & mine). / My face has never been a place to hide / I say to his future scar, but now / people can see between my eyes / what lines I feel / with swollen morning fingers, hands / I never noticed aging until ache. / My dog touches his toes to the ground / barks at the breeze on our first post-surgery walk / to scream he is still here still / throwing himself against his fears / while I shade my eyes, deep punctuated / sadness I can no longer pretend / never happened / or the world cannot see.

Holocene Sonnet

i)   The bloom—the pretty part we want—is
ii)   often how a threatened plant screams *help*.
iii)   Venus flytraps can be sedated.
iv)   Therefore, they can wake & be made calm.
v)   Lice hatch ravenous for blood & claw
vi)   linoleum one foot per minute.
vii)   Mammoth sunflowers reseeded
viii)   from previous diseased seasons sing
ix)   the same sickness for generations.
x)   Pepsis wasps haul tarantulas up
xi)   mountainsides to provide warm
xii)   meals for larvae. Imagine children
xiii)   dragging men across highway lanes
xiv)   to eat them alive, thigh by thigh.

Guy & Realdoll

Claudia, he coos, & switches her tongue
to the one for speaking. They're jealous,
he thinks, an eye half to the world,
& crosses her legs on the park
bench. Joggers & suits rubberneck
to check her for breath. *Nope*,
one sniggers & turns back to an iPhone.
Of course she spoke before his hand moved
up her shirt, up what passes for spine, before he
gave her the name she'd wear for life.

If the best art is that which conceals art,
why would anyone question Claudia's kiss,
that her deft steps & red stilettos
can make a man weep? It's not just
the curve of her leg, the bulb her calf makes
when strained by an arch, the way
her toes strangle to breathe. For him,
her olive dress hemmed to the knee, the breath
he's left at that bend in her leg, to feel her flesh
push back is all he needs to rise. But to spoon

her—with an arm around a globe of his own
making—would be to pool her blood for worship.
And now it comes, he says, *that distant applause*,
as rain begins to needle through the park. Wind

shifts & spins her head to a world over his
shoulder. She says nothing. *But Claudia,* he coos
& switches her tongue to the one for kissing.
I'm so happy, he says, the sky concrete, women
click-clacking by like mannequins, his heart
so whole the trees let go their plastic.

ACOA Questionnaire

1) *What is an ACOA?*

My first love's father was wearing
a strange lady's bra over his shirt
when we came home drunk & went
to bed together at sixteen years old.
He said, tilting his head toward
my chest, Don't need more than
a mouthful anyway, son. Sleep well.

2) *Do my parents need to be alcoholics?*

At least once every day, I practice
in my bathroom mirror both sides
of the hypothetical argument I plan
to have with a stranger or love interest.
At night, I lie in bed certain the world's
largest sinkhole is located directly below
my home that has stood here eighty years
but will be consumed during my tenancy.

3) *What is the cost?*

My second love's father struggled
to balance himself on a bucket to see
through the window while I peed.
Later he kissed me hard on the mouth
twice, for birthing his son's son (my
own dad there—disgusted though
smirking toward my best friend's
camel toe). Oh, boys—

4) *What is a Higher Power?*

don't look at me like I don't know
a boner often accompanies a hug.
Let me never neglect the third
love—tender, intelligent, & better
at convincing me that our professor
was not studying the curve of my ass.

5) *Can I attend a Closed Meeting?*

This isn't just for uncles who run
their palms up a girl's sickbed
while her dad's out of town
& her mother is not yet dead
drunk but she's not home either.

6) *Where is a meeting?*

Blackout doesn't mean forget.
A brain simply stops making memories.
Where was your mother? Where's the girl
who can do the worm, who shoots eggs
in haystacks, who gets nervous & kazoos
with her mouth the entire "Wreck
of the Edmund Fitzgerald."

7) *How do I find a meeting when there are none in my area?*

What of the sun dumping
through the bay window turns
days to years & what's remembered
can't be forgotten but what can't be
recalled won't let go. Who no longer
knows her only sister's address. Who
holds the bulb to a poisonous plant
can't refuse chewing with both hands.

If You Just Remember the Good Times

it gets easier, meaning *stop fucking crying already*.
Why is it never enough that your dad tried

to drown your mother in the bathtub
when she was eight months pregnant

with you. Never enough to hate you both.
Another summer. Another chance to sow

a wall of mammoths around another house
you won't call home. Tell the bees your fear

is constant but not about them. Some lost
belonging inside your dog's body calls him

to howl for the sound of every passing
ambulance. Now we are all unlearning

what it means to be safe. We are alone
by design, you remind the stunted girl

you were & the woman you're becoming
laughs. She knows, like any cunning hero

starring in his own myth, you were never
really fighting to find home. Who cares

if the lullaby's a muted wish, if you don't
want to remember good times. You don't

want gods to love you but to make you more
of what a hawk is. You want cigarettes

to be nutritious. Want this body not to forget
warm skin in its hands—blood summoned

by some site of impact. You hazardous land,
bees born of a corpse is what your love needs.

In Love, Fridays are Best Spent Watching the Discovery Channel

In the Riverine Forest of Serengeti, siafu roll their dark tide highway toward acacias and black mane lions. A sisterhood—twenty-two million strong—unified in a hunt for breath. According to myrmecologists, ants make up one third of the planet's animal weight, and these are the harvesters of flesh. They bridge into every orifice, asphyxiate and devour a frog in under an hour, polish a cow's bones within two weeks. Nothing cleans meat from a skull like siafu. When it's time, these sirens sing their pheromone song to the sausage fly. Mature enough to need, he'll stagger into the swarm of sentries who tear him wingless and bring him to the queen of trees and grasslands. He is mated once before eaten. Only the Masai understand the matriarchy of siafu. How they rid a crop square of insects and rats in seconds flat. How their man-eating pincers double as sutures. Even after their bodies are pulled from their heads, they still hold on, closing the wound.

Love Apology

I knew when you walked out
        of that bathroom, when I first
                saw your face, the same

way I've always known death
        is nothing to fear. I once read
                a book about face shapes

betraying who we really are
        though I didn't need to read it
                to see the kindness in your eyes

is something I learned long ago
        to run from. Always have been
                the days when I needed a man

to wield my secrets as weapons
        against me, until I learned to be mean
                enough to myself. Grief's gift

to me is knowing life can be lived
        in readying for the end without
                forgetting the present is built

inside it. I raised one hundred sunflowers
          & passed their seeds to my son, hoping
              he would sow & harvest them

year after year, so his son could know
          my eyes even once I'm whole again.
              I love the earth is not the lie.

I need to tell my son I was once
          a jar of untumbled broken
              glass is not the excuse

for taking his face between my hands
          & screaming like a small girl lost
              in a smoke-filled kitchen.

She was who I wasn't but where I was
          & now, remembering I'm a woman
              feeling deeply, I don't know how

to let myself try again. Who could
          trust me to hold such stained glass
              & hope the sun angles through.

Where the Bottom Dropped Out

You picked him up

by his head

[insert fact about young brain stem
you can't make yourself
look up].

Say it again. That's not who you are
but

where you were.

You left her body

on a colorless

table.

Sign your name. [pen] Sign again.

You picked him up

as if he was already

pieces.

[extubation: 1) your name's tangled cursive suffering such severely straight lines]

He pulled the tube from her body   You picked him up by his head
like siphoning gas   like control
a machine that reminds you   you will never let go
air is the power   you will never forgive
yourself

The Trying

For weeks I repeat *write the loneliness poem*, but I can't pinpoint the last time someone touched my shoulders. I don't know what song played during the first sex I didn't want, even if I can't call it what it was. My body does, & it refuses to remember. The older I get the harder I have to try to want to stay alive. Columns of sun cut the cumulus raw. I walk my dog on garbage day & cry for the volume of waste we produce each week. For the squirrel, the bird, the baby bunny flattened to asphalt as if it was never anything else. I shoot a loogie at a *No Joe & his Hoe* yard sign, where a guy cut & taped paper letters **TRUMP 2024** to his front window. These white guys frighten me more than any creature living or dead since they believe they still own me, circling the blocks in their pickups, nodding & grinning like their cigarettes know my skin or will. I don't need to feel adored, but what I'd give to simply be understood. My tallest sunflowers are telling me it's finally time to let them

go, their leaves browning, their heads
begging for the comfort of ground
though I'm so afraid to say goodbye
to the walls they've grown around me.

What Burning We Are,
What Water We Want

for RBG

Your death let the what-if in so those men
gathered hoodless but hunting & not a bird

had fallen from the sky not for all the fire
skipping rivers & roads but women bunched

their shirts into knots at their throats knowing
the if was already answered so we were waiting

for the when to butterfly blade our uncrossed
legs clean of that which offends. Every woman

has been running toward death in the same burning
dress down the same road lined with the same men

made mostly of water. Every one of them a weapon
if they're never held right. The history of puppetry

hinges on the ability of one to manipulate many
inanimate objects to create the illusion they're alive.

Through the window of this first morning without
you, my sunflowers read vacant. It keeps me inside

for days. It's hard to see what seems like death

protecting life. I confused bowing for weakness

slender bent necks never breaking, making futures
safe from rain & faces.

                    Men have been every hurt
worked—seeds raising bombs through dirt.

Now is not the time to be caught
                         crying in my purse.

Sheltering in Place,

despite viral memes, never actually meant
      giraffes or deer were reclaiming city streets

though the oldest tiger at the Bronx Zoo was
      infected too & Earth was quaking more

frequently it seemed (but wasn't she always
      speaking clearly at a table full of men

who couldn't hear Her over them). Listen—
      there is not a single living witness here

who understands her entire violent existence.
      It happens this way—you wake at 4:53 a.m.

to learn that your father, like your mother,
      died in a strange bathroom & you're forty

living alone discovering your dead parents
      took the earliest version of you with them.

No breathing being remembers you little now.
      You begin to envy people who believe

in God as their witness, even if he mumbles
      so low it doesn't matter if you turn

the music down. I'd like to trust we will see
   our hands new now & hold each other

less like poison berries, but I've walked my dog
   around the block past the same house

that sat empty so long it was all but mine
   & when some couple wedged a love seat

through the narrow door I eyed them like I
   would any threat. Maybe we've each spent

too much time in the room of ourselves
   that likes pain, repeating *once this is*

over, wearing our makeshift masks, waiting
   for our faces to grow into them.

As Vulture

It's probably impossible for me to help
you see me as every purifying breeze

breathed into a body built to fight the fall
that each of us is falling. I can smell death

a mile away. Every day. All day. It calls so
I rise high as planes & soar hours without

beating a wing. Of course I envy eagle
talons & the crow's cross voice. I'm bald

headed & ready to bury myself neck up
for any flesh in need. Praise carrion

its soft pockets & orifices. Praise this
hooked beak, really. Praise for pissing

acid on my feet before I eat, for shitting
myself for warmth, for puking on my kids

when they anger me. I'm spreading nothing
but *now I lay me down to sleep* over an earth

devouring itself with disease. I'm my own
solar panel. I dwell instead of nest. I kettle

spiral down ribs of cloud, punctuating a sky
that never tells. Don't bother asking why

I too am steadfast in this hunger. It comes
from within or to or for us all & never

surrenders. I'm waiting patiently for you
to stop walking, to scrape clean your needs

against parched dirt under a punishing sun
so we can both be absolved of our answers.

Letter to November 3, 2020

On second thought, in the autopsy
of this world, no animal will speak
of people. My need, my friend

claims, to say people instead
of us is psychopathic or at least
the bottles in the broken water

are wet. My lovelife was a praying
mantis this summer. So what.
Grammatically speaking, I believe trees

will grieve only once
we are gone completely.
I wish they'd tell me how far away

they can hear each other speak
or scream or if the squirrels can reach
their frequency. I want to feel Earth

working through me never meant
I hope my chest would churn a pile
of knives, but elections, like primary

colors, are terrifying. Who said birds
believe in goodness. Stay in line.
I hope some brain out there does

know how long I stared at your smile
next to your ex-wife's on Facebook
every night after the night you iced

your gum from my hair & cried
before kissing me, burying your
flowers blossoms down. Show me

when humans weren't like—this
is a scary fucking time to be alive.
Now, like then, are when my words

could get me burned. In an actual blaze.
Attached to a large piece of blameless tree.
In the middle of a bustling street of us.

Why to Feel the Host

The day Brazil went black at noon
everyone could see their hands

around Earth's throat, their finger
bruises up her wide thighs, so they did

all they knew to do with such darkness
& the streets filled with headlights.

Scientists have prepared by starting
a self-propelling heart in a jar. Already

the nose grows in its dish. A planet
can make its star wobble. Humans refuse

to feel Earth's hurt—sirens she sends—
shortness of breath, pain in our chests,

sweaty impending senses of doom we
muzzle inside us. We believe breathing

love into each other's love isn't fighting
fire with air. We drug then count ourselves

lucky to worry less, not to wear the terror
of her noose. So she'll raze us. Not with flame

or wind or wave but human hate—the way
a parasite drives an ant to balance on a blade

of grass, sacrificing itself to a progress
it can't understand. A planet won't

wait for love to free her from being
everyone's everything. She's convinced

men the world is theirs, so those abusers—
eaten or burned—will volunteer to leave her

alone so she can tend the cliffsides that were
always Her. Then, the vultures will show

how quiet the world was before us
& the trees will never tell the story

of the people who once sang to cover
the sound of the one who was leaving,

who might sleep cold but under open sky
that night. Clear your throat. Get ready.

Notes

The italicized lines in "Synthetic Love" are plucked and paraphrased from dialogue in the documentary *Guys and Dolls*.

The title and some italicized lines in "September 1, 2019," are from/allude to W. H. Auden's poem "September 1, 1939," and some language in this crown comes straight from 45's face, as well as Weather.com and Wikipedia.com.

In "Crown," the line "say you down through time" owes its existence to William Heyen's prose poem/flash essay "The Host."

The last line in "Sheltering in Place," nods to George Orwell.

Acknowledgments

Academy of American Poets *Poem-a-Day*: "Holocene Sonnet"
Barrelhouse: "Synthetic Love"
Birmingham Poetry Review: "A Son Might Say" & "Crown"
Copper Nickel: "Why to Save the World"*
Glass: A Journal of Poetry: "In Love, Fridays Are Best Spent Watching the
    Discovery Channel"
Gulf Coast: "Anxiety"*
The Missouri Review: "Oubliette"
Ocean State Review: "ACOA Questionnaire" & "Love Apology"
Sewanee Theological Review: "Guy & Realdoll"
South Dakota Review: "The Killing Game" & "Learning Not To Want"
Terrain: "Letter to the Aftermath"
Waxwing: "To the Friend Who Sent Me Goodwill Forks as a Gift"*
I-70 Review: "As Vulture" & "Sheltering in Place,"

*"Anxiety" was selected by Natalie Diaz as the winner of the 2021 *Gulf Coast*
    Poetry Prize.

*"Why to Save the World" and "To the Friend Who Sent Me Goodwill
    Forks as a Gift" were nominated for Pushcart Prizes in 2020.

Endless gratitude to the friends, poets, and colleagues who were early readers
of this work, as well as those folks who supported these poems or who buoyed
me while I delved into this difficult content: Lillian-Yvonne Bertram, John
Gibler, Trey Moody, Chloe Honum, Emily Borgmann, and Diane Seuss. I'm
grateful to poet Ilya Kaminsky for being genuine, generous, and inspiring in

our conversations during his visit to Omaha, which led to this collection's opening poem, and to the University of Nebraska at Omaha for making such interactions possible and for granting me the gift of time, by way of a Faculty Development Fellowship, which allowed me to cinch this manuscript.

Thank you, Jesse Lee Kercheval and Sean Bishop, for putting your faith in this book, selecting it for inclusion in the Wisconsin Poetry Series, and to everyone at the University of Wisconsin Press for bringing this collection to life. As a University of Wisconsin–Green Bay alum, having this book published with UW Press feels very special. And to every reader, especially trauma survivors and/or those actively mourning or fighting the trauma inflicted on our planet, thank you for holding these poems with me.

Lisa Fay Coutley is the author of *tether* (2020); *Errata* (2015), winner of the Crab Orchard Series in Poetry Open Competition; *In the Carnival of Breathing* (2011), winner of the Black River Chapbook Competition; and *Small Girl* (2024). She is the editor of the anthology *In the Tempered Dark: Contemporary Poets Transcending Elegy* (2024). Her poetry has been awarded an NEA Fellowship; an Academy of American Poets Levis Prize, chosen by Dana Levin; and the 2021 *Gulf Coast* Poetry Prize, selected by Natalie Diaz. Recent prose and poetry appears in the Academy of American Poets *Poem-a-Day*, *Barrelhouse*, *Brevity*, *Copper Nickel*, and *Gulf Coast*. She is an associate professor of poetry and creative nonfiction in the Writer's Workshop at the University of Nebraska at Omaha, where she advises the campus journal, and she is the Chapbook Series Editor at Black Lawrence Press.

(B) = Winner of the Brittingham Prize in Poetry
(FP) = Winner of the Felix Pollak Prize in Poetry
(4L) = Winner of the Four Lakes Prize in Poetry
(T) = Winner of the Wisconsin Prize for Poetry in Translation

The Low End of Higher Things • David Clewell

Now We're Getting Somewhere (FP) • David Clewell

Taken Somehow by Surprise (4L) • David Clewell

Thunderhead • Emily Rose Cole

Borrowed Dress (FP) • Cathy Colman

Host • Lisa Fay Coutley

Dear Terror, Dear Splendor • Melissa Crowe

Places/Everyone (B) • Jim Daniels

Show and Tell • Jim Daniels

Darkroom (B) • Jazzy Danziger

And Her Soul Out of Nothing (B) • Olena Kalytiak Davis

Afterlife (FP) • Michael Dhyne

My Favorite Tyrants (B) • Joanne Diaz

Midwhistle • Dante Di Stefano

Talking to Strangers (B) • Patricia Dobler

Alien Miss • Carlina Duan

The Golden Coin (4L) • Alan Feldman

Immortality (4L) • Alan Feldman

A Sail to Great Island (FP) • Alan Feldman

Psalms • Julia Fiedorczuk, translated by Bill Johnston

The Word We Used for It (B) • Max Garland

A Field Guide to the Heavens (B) • Frank X. Gaspar

The Royal Baker's Daughter (FP) • Barbara Goldberg

Fractures (FP) • Carlos Andrés Gómez

Gloss • Rebecca Hazelton

Funny (FP) • Jennifer Michael Hecht

Queen in Blue • Ambalila Hemsell

How to Kill a Goat & Other Monsters • Saúl Hernández

The Legend of Light (FP) • Bob Hicok

Sweet Ruin (B) • Tony Hoagland

House of Sparrows: New and Selected Poems (4L) • Betsy Sholl
Late Psalm • Betsy Sholl
Otherwise Unseeable (4L) • Betsy Sholl
Blood Work (FP) • Matthew Siegel
Fruit (4L) • Bruce Snider
The Year We Studied Women (FP) • Bruce Snider
Bird Skin Coat (B) • Angela Sorby
The Sleeve Waves (FP) • Angela Sorby
If the House (B) • Molly Spencer
Wait (B) • Alison Stine
Hive (B) • Christina Stoddard
The Red Virgin: A Poem of Simone Weil (B) • Stephanie Strickland
The Room Where I Was Born (B) • Brian Teare
Fragments in Us: Recent and Earlier Poems (FP) • Dennis Trudell
Girl's Guide to Leaving • Laura Villareal
The Apollonia Poems (4L) • Judith Vollmer
Level Green (B) • Judith Vollmer
Reactor • Judith Vollmer
The Sound Boat: New and Selected Poems (4L) • Judith Vollmer
Voodoo Inverso (FP) • Mark Wagenaar
Hot Popsicles • Charles Harper Webb
Liver (FP) • Charles Harper Webb
The Blue Hour (B) • Jennifer Whitaker
American Sex Tape (B) • Jameka Williams
Centaur (B) • Greg Wrenn
Pocket Sundial (B) • Lisa Zeidner